ATIRAXIA

AI Made Very Simple

A Begginer's Guide to Understanding Artificial Intelligence

Atiraxia

Contents

Chapter 1: What Is AI and Why Should You Care?

Artificial Intelligence, or AI, is something you probably hear about all the time. It's in the news, in movies, in the gadgets we use every day. But despite how much it's talked about, many people still don't really know what AI actually is, or why it should matter to them. AI isn't just for tech experts or the future; it's something that's already changing the way we live, work, and interact with technology. From the simple tasks we rely on every day, like setting a reminder with Siri, to more complex systems, like self-driving cars, AI is becoming more and more a part of our lives.

At its core, AI refers to machines or software that can perform tasks that would usually require human intelligence. But here's the thing: it's not about building robots that think and feel like us, but about creating systems that can process information and learn from it to improve over time. So, think of AI as being about making machines smarter—able to understand, adapt, and do things like recognize faces in photos, make predictions based on data, or even help doctors diagnose diseases. The really exciting part is that it can do all this without needing a human to program it for every possible situation. It learns from examples, gets better with time, and can do a lot of things much faster and more efficiently than people.

You're probably already interacting with AI without even thinking about it. When you open an app like Facebook, it suggests friends or pages you might like. When you use Google, it predicts what you want to search for based on the first few words you type. These are all forms of AI that help make your digital experience easier and more personalized. Even when you use your phone's camera, it's likely using AI to improve your photos—adjusting the lighting, focusing on faces, and identifying objects in the background.

AI in Everyday Life

AI doesn't just work behind the scenes; it's part of your daily routine. Whether you're checking social media, shopping online, or using voice assistants, AI is quietly improving your experiences. But these are just the basics. Let's look at a few ways AI is making your life simpler without you even realizing it.

When you ask your phone to play your favorite song, or tell it to remind you of an appointment, you're using AI. The voice assistants on your smartphone—like Siri, Google Assistant, or Alexa—use AI to understand what you're saying and respond in a way that makes sense. They do this by analyzing your words, comparing them to vast databases of information, and then determining the best possible response. It's like having a conversation with someone who's always learning how to understand you better.

Then, there are **recommendation systems**. Have you ever opened Netflix and noticed that it suggests shows or movies based on what you've watched before? Or scrolled through Amazon and seen products recommended just for you? That's AI making predictions based on the data it has about your past behavior. AI systems analyze your viewing or shopping habits and predict what you might like next. It's like having a personal assistant who remembers your preferences and helps guide you to the next thing you'll enjoy.

AI is also getting smarter in things like **self-driving cars**. Although we don't have fully autonomous vehicles on the road everywhere just yet, AI is already working in cars to make driving safer and easier. Features like automatic emergency braking, lane-keeping assist, and adaptive cruise control all use AI to help drivers make better decisions in real-time. This is just the beginning. In the future, self-driving cars could change the way we think about transportation, making travel safer, faster, and more efficient.

Why Should You Care About AI?

If AI is already all around you, it's important to understand why it's something you should care about. Even if you're not a techie, understanding AI can make a big difference in how you interact with technology and how it impacts your daily life.

1. **AI is Changing Industries**: From healthcare to finance, AI is transforming how industries operate. It's helping doctors diagnose diseases more accurately, allowing businesses to predict customer behavior, and even making cars smarter. AI isn't just a novelty; it's helping solve complex problems and make processes more efficient.

2. **AI Improves Your Life**: Whether it's making your digital experiences more personalized or helping with everyday tasks, AI is making life more convenient. It's already part of how you work, shop, and communicate. By understanding AI, you can get even more out of these tools and use them to your advantage.

3. **AI Raises Ethical Questions**: While AI has a lot of benefits, it also comes with challenges. As AI systems make decisions, they raise important ethical questions. How can we ensure that AI is fair? How do we make sure AI systems don't have biases or make decisions that hurt people? These are questions that everyone should be thinking about as AI becomes more prevalent.

4. **AI Will Shape the Future of Work**: AI is already changing the job market. Some jobs may be replaced by machines, but others will be created. As AI continues to evolve, new opportunities will arise in fields like AI development, robotics, and data science. By understanding how AI works, you can prepare yourself for the future of work and make sure you're ready to take advantage of these new opportunities.

AI in the Media vs. Real Life

When we watch movies or read books about AI, it often seems like the technology is much more advanced than it really is. In movies, AI is often portrayed as a kind of super-intelligent force, capable of doing anything and even becoming self-aware. In reality, AI is much less dramatic and far more practical. Sure, there's potential for AI to grow in complexity, but we're still a long way from creating machines that think and feel like humans.

Right now, most AI is what's called **narrow AI**. This means it's designed to perform a specific task, like recognizing speech or diagnosing a disease. It doesn't have a general understanding of the world or emotions like humans do. AI today is incredibly powerful, but it's also limited—it's great at certain things, but it can't do everything. For example, the AI that powers a self-driving car is amazing at processing data about the road, but it can't make complex decisions in the same way a human driver can. Similarly, AI that helps recommend products on Amazon doesn't "understand" what a product is or why you might like it; it simply recognizes patterns in your shopping history and predicts what you might want next.

This difference is important to understand because it helps us think about the future of AI more realistically. While AI has immense potential, it's still a tool—albeit a very powerful one—that can help us solve problems and improve efficiency. And even though movies make it seem like AI could one day become a conscious entity; that's still a long way off.

How AI Works

At this point, you might be thinking, "Okay, AI sounds cool, but how does it actually work?" That's a great question. To understand how AI works, we need to break it down into a few basic concepts: **machine learning**, **data**, and **algorithms**. These are the core building blocks that allow AI systems to function and improve over time.

Machine Learning is a branch of AI that focuses on teaching machines how to learn from data. Instead of programming a machine to follow a set of specific instructions for every possible situation, we let it learn from examples. Imagine teaching a child to recognize animals by showing them pictures. Over time, the child learns to associate certain features—like the shape of a dog's ears or the color of a cat's fur—with the correct animal. In the same way, an AI system learns to identify patterns in data, gradually improving its ability to make decisions.

One of the simplest forms of machine learning is called **supervised learning**, which is like giving the system a set of labeled examples. For example, if you wanted to train an AI to recognize cats and dogs, you'd show it thousands of labeled images—some marked as "cat" and others as "dog." The AI would analyze these images, learning to associate features like fur texture, ear shape, and nose type with the correct label. Over time, it gets better at identifying cats and dogs in new, unlabeled images.

Another important part of how AI works is **data**. You might have heard the phrase, "data is the new oil," and there's a reason for that. AI systems rely on vast amounts of data to learn and improve. The more data they have, the better they can recognize patterns and make predictions. For example, a recommendation system on a streaming platform like Netflix uses data about your viewing history—along with the behavior of other users—to suggest shows and movies you might like.

The more data it has, the more accurate and personalized its recommendations become.

Finally, there are **algorithms**, which are the step-by-step instructions that tell the AI how to process the data and make decisions. Think of algorithms as the recipes AI uses to turn raw ingredients (data) into a finished dish (a prediction or decision). These algorithms are designed to process data efficiently, recognize patterns, and adjust over time as the AI gets better.

Types of AI

AI isn't just a single technology—it's actually made up of different types, each with its own strengths and limitations. Let's look at the three main types of AI that are most commonly discussed: **Narrow AI**, **General AI**, and **Superintelligent AI**.

1. **Narrow AI (Weak AI)**: This is the type of AI that we see all around us today. Narrow AI is designed to perform a specific task—like recognizing faces, recommending products, or translating languages. It's highly specialized and does one thing very well, but it's not capable of doing anything beyond that specific task. For example, the AI in your phone's camera is great at recognizing faces, but it can't do things like read a book or drive a car. Narrow AI is everywhere, powering everything from social media platforms to search engines and self-checkout machines at stores.

2. **General AI (Strong AI)**: General AI is still mostly theoretical, and it's what people often think of when they imagine "true" AI. This is the kind of AI that could perform any intellectual task that a human can do. General AI would be able to think, reason, and understand in the same way that humans do, and it could transfer its learning from one area to another.

For example, if a general AI learned how to play chess, it could apply that knowledge to learn how to play other games, or even solve completely unrelated problems. While we're still far from creating general AI, it's something that researchers are actively working toward.

3. **Superintelligent AI**: Superintelligent AI is the stuff of science fiction, but it's often discussed as the next step after general AI. A superintelligent AI would not only be able to perform any intellectual task that a human can do, but it would also exceed human intelligence in every way. It would be able to solve problems, innovate, and learn at a pace and depth far beyond what any human could achieve. While superintelligent AI remains a concept for the future, it raises important ethical questions about how such powerful technology should be controlled and used.

For now, **Narrow AI** is the type of AI that's most relevant to our everyday lives. It's what powers things like voice assistants, spam filters, and recommendation engines. But as AI continues to advance, the line between narrow and general AI is becoming blurrier, and we're seeing more applications where AI can handle a broader range of tasks. Understanding the different types of AI can help you see where the technology is now and where it might be headed.

Why AI Matters to You

AI isn't just a buzzword—it's shaping the future of everything from how we interact with technology to how industries operate. Understanding AI is important for anyone who wants to be part of this rapidly evolving landscape. Here are a few reasons why AI matters to you:

1. **AI Makes Things Easier**: From personalized recommendations to smart home devices, AI is designed to make your life easier. It learns your preferences and adapts to your needs, whether it's suggesting movies or adjusting the thermostat in your home. As AI continues to improve, it will only become more integrated into the tools and services you use every day.

2. **AI Changes the Way We Work**: AI is already transforming industries and the workforce. In fields like healthcare, AI is helping doctors make more accurate diagnoses. In finance, it's improving how we analyze market trends and detect fraud. AI is automating many repetitive tasks, but it's also creating new job opportunities in fields like data science, AI development, and robotics. The more you understand AI, the better prepared you'll be to adapt to the changing job market.

3. **AI Raises Ethical Issues**: With all the power that AI brings, it also raises important questions. How do we ensure that AI systems are fair and unbiased? How do we protect our privacy in an age where AI systems can access so much personal data? Understanding these issues is crucial as AI becomes more embedded in society, and it will be up to all of us to make sure it's used responsibly.

4. **AI Will Shape the Future**: The potential for AI to solve problems is enormous. From curing diseases to solving environmental challenges, AI could help address some of the world's most pressing issues. But it also brings challenges that we need to address, such as job displacement and ethical concerns. By understanding AI, you can be part of the conversation about how we should use this technology to shape a better future.

The Future of AI

As AI continues to evolve, its impact will only grow, shaping more aspects of our world in ways we can't fully predict yet. The future of AI is often discussed in terms of its potential to solve complex problems, enhance human capabilities, and revolutionize entire industries. But while AI brings immense opportunities, it also comes with challenges and ethical dilemmas that need to be addressed. So, what does the future look like, and why should you care?

AI and the Changing Job Market

One of the most talked-about aspects of AI's future is its impact on the job market. As AI becomes more sophisticated, it's expected to automate many tasks that humans currently do, particularly in industries like manufacturing, customer service, and transportation. In fact, some studies predict that millions of jobs will be replaced by AI and automation in the coming decades. While this may sound alarming, it's important to remember that AI isn't just about replacing jobs—it's also about **creating new opportunities**.

New roles in fields like AI development, data analysis, and robotics are already emerging, and as AI continues to improve, even more opportunities will be created. However, this means that workers will need to adapt by learning new skills and staying updated on the latest technologies. The future of work will likely involve a collaboration between humans and AI, where humans handle tasks that require creativity, empathy, and judgment, while AI handles repetitive or data-intensive tasks.

For instance, while AI can analyze vast amounts of data much faster than a human could, it still lacks the creativity and emotional intelligence needed for tasks like artistic creation or complex decision-making in uncertain environments. The key to navigating this future will be ensuring that workers are equipped with the skills needed to thrive in an AI-driven world.

AI in Healthcare: A Revolution in Medicine

The potential of AI in healthcare is one of the most exciting prospects for the future. AI systems are already helping doctors make more accurate diagnoses by analyzing medical data faster and more efficiently than humans can. For example, AI has been used to detect signs of diseases like cancer in medical images, sometimes even outperforming doctors in terms of speed and accuracy. This could lead to earlier diagnoses and better outcomes for patients.

But AI's potential goes beyond just diagnostics. It's also being used to **personalize treatments** for patients based on their unique genetic makeup, lifestyle, and medical history. AI is helping researchers analyze vast amounts of genetic and clinical data to identify potential treatments for diseases like cancer and Alzheimer's. This could lead to more targeted, effective treatments that are tailored to individual patients, rather than the "one-size-fits-all" approach we've seen in the past.

Additionally, AI is being used in the development of **drug discovery**. AI can sift through vast amounts of research data, finding patterns and connections that humans might miss, helping to identify new drug candidates more quickly and efficiently. This could significantly speed up the process of finding new treatments, which is especially important for diseases that currently have no cure.

AI and Transportation: The Road to Autonomous Vehicles

Self-driving cars are often the first thing people think about

11

when they hear about AI in transportation, and it's easy to see why. The idea of cars that can drive themselves without human intervention is both exciting and a little daunting. But while we're still a few years away from fully autonomous vehicles being commonplace, AI is already having a significant impact on the transportation industry.

In addition to self-driving cars, AI is being used to **improve traffic management**. AI systems can analyze real-time traffic data to optimize traffic lights, reduce congestion, and improve overall traffic flow. This not only makes driving more efficient but also reduces fuel consumption and pollution, contributing to a greener, more sustainable future.

Moreover, AI is helping to make **public transportation** more efficient. Cities are using AI to analyze traffic patterns and optimize bus and train schedules, ensuring that they run more efficiently and arrive on time. This is especially useful in large cities where public transportation systems can become overcrowded and inefficient. As AI continues to improve, we can expect even more innovative solutions to transform how we get around.

AI Ethics: Navigating the Challenges

While the future of AI is exciting, it also raises important **ethical questions** that need to be addressed. AI has the potential to solve some of the world's most pressing problems, but it also has the power to exacerbate existing inequalities if not used responsibly. One of the main concerns with AI is **bias**. AI systems are only as good as the data they are trained on, and if that data reflects biases—whether it's based on race, gender, or socioeconomic status—the AI will reflect those biases in its decisions. For example, if an AI system is trained on data that's biased against certain groups of people, it could make unfair decisions in areas like hiring or law enforcement.

Another ethical issue is **privacy**. AI systems often rely on vast amounts of personal data to function, whether it's tracking your location, analyzing your browsing habits, or even monitoring your health. This raises important questions about how this data is used and who has access to it. We need to ensure that AI systems are designed to protect user privacy and that people have control over their own data.

Lastly, there's the issue of **job displacement**. As AI automates more tasks, there's a risk that many jobs will be replaced by machines. While some jobs will be created, others will disappear, and this could have significant social and economic consequences. It's crucial that we find ways to ensure that workers are not left behind in an AI-driven world. This may involve investing in education and training programs that help people learn the skills they need to thrive in a rapidly changing job market.

The Path Forward: Ensuring Responsible AI

As we look to the future of AI, it's important that we don't just focus on the potential benefits but also address the challenges and risks that come with it. Ensuring that AI is used responsibly and ethically will require collaboration between governments, businesses, researchers, and the public. This means creating regulations that promote fairness, transparency, and accountability in AI systems.

We also need to ensure that **AI is inclusive**—that it benefits everyone, not just a select few. This means making sure that diverse voices are involved in the development of AI technologies and that AI systems are trained on diverse data to avoid perpetuating biases. As AI continues to grow and evolve, it will be up to all of us to ensure that it is used for the greater good, solving problems and creating opportunities for people all over the world.

The future of AI is bright, but it's also complex. By understanding how AI works, why it's important, and the challenges it brings, we can better prepare for the changes it will bring to our lives and our world. AI is not just a technology for the future—it's here, and it's already changing the way we live. It's up to us to make sure that it's used in ways that are ethical, inclusive, and beneficial to all.

The Impact of AI on Everyday Decisions

While AI might seem like a complicated or futuristic technology, it's actually influencing many of the decisions you make every day, often in ways that are subtle and seamless. From the moment you wake up to when you go to bed, AI is quietly shaping your daily routine, whether you're aware of it or not.

One of the most significant ways AI affects us is through **personalization**. You've likely noticed that when you browse the web, shop online, or even scroll through social media, the content presented to you seems tailored to your tastes. Whether it's a suggestion for a new book on Amazon or a video recommended by YouTube, AI is behind these decisions. AI algorithms analyze your behavior—what you click on, what you watch, what you buy—and then make predictions about what you might like next. Over time, these systems become better at personalizing content, providing you with experiences that feel unique to your preferences.

Similarly, **AI in search engines** is designed to provide more accurate results based on what you're likely looking for.

The search engine uses AI to understand the context of your query, how you worded it, and how similar searches have been answered in the past. Whether you're searching for a recipe, the latest news, or a product to buy, AI ensures that the results you see are as relevant as possible.

Even something as simple as **smart recommendations** can be powered by AI. Streaming services like Netflix, Spotify, and Hulu use AI to recommend movies, shows, or music based on your viewing or listening habits. These services analyze patterns across millions of users, helping you discover content that matches your interests. This kind of personalization doesn't just stop at entertainment—it's even used in news feeds to keep you updated on topics you care about, whether that's sports, politics, or hobbies.

AI's Role in Social Media

Another area where AI has a profound impact is in **social media**. Social media platforms like Facebook, Instagram, and Twitter rely on AI to curate the content that appears in your feed. This isn't just about showing you the latest posts from your friends—it's about predicting what you're most likely to engage with. The AI takes into account your past activity, including what you've liked, shared, or commented on, and uses this data to suggest posts you'll find interesting.

AI also plays a role in **content moderation**. With billions of posts being shared every day, it's impossible for humans to monitor every piece of content in real-time. AI systems help identify inappropriate or harmful content—like hate speech, graphic violence, or misinformation—and remove or flag it for review. This technology is still improving, but it's a critical part of keeping social media spaces safe and user-friendly.

Interestingly, AI also helps determine what ads you see while scrolling through social media. Advertisers use AI to create more targeted ad campaigns, ensuring their ads reach people who are most likely to be interested in their products. If you've ever bought something online and then noticed ads for similar products following you around the web, that's AI at work, using your browsing history to target ads based on your interests.

AI's Influence on Creativity and Art

While AI is commonly associated with automation and efficiency, it's also making waves in the world of **creativity**. AI is being used to assist in the creation of art, music, writing, and even design. For instance, there are AI programs that can generate artwork in the style of famous artists or create music that sounds similar to a specific genre. These AI tools are not replacing human creativity but are providing new ways for people to express themselves and explore artistic possibilities.

In writing, AI is being used to help create stories, articles, and even poetry. AI writing assistants, like the one you're using right now, can help you brainstorm ideas, improve your writing, or even generate entire paragraphs based on a prompt. While this technology is still developing, it holds a lot of potential for writers, journalists, and content creators. It's not about replacing human authors, but offering them new tools to assist in the creative process.

In the **design world**, AI is helping artists and designers come up with fresh ideas for everything from fashion to interior design. AI tools can analyze trends, predict what's likely to be popular in the future, and even generate design ideas based on a set of parameters. This collaboration between AI and human creativity is opening up exciting new possibilities for innovation in art and design.

AI and Ethical Challenges

As AI becomes more embedded in our lives, it brings with it a range of **ethical challenges**. One of the biggest concerns with AI is its **potential for bias**. Since AI systems learn from data, if the data they're trained on is biased, the AI will reflect those biases in its decisions. For example, if an AI system is trained on biased data from the past—such as hiring practices that favored one gender or race over another—the system might continue to make biased decisions in the future, perpetuating existing inequalities.

There have been cases where AI systems used for hiring or criminal justice have demonstrated biased outcomes. For example, AI tools used in hiring might favor male candidates over female candidates, even if both have the same qualifications. Similarly, AI systems used to predict recidivism in the criminal justice system have been shown to disproportionately target minority groups. These biases can have serious consequences, which is why there's a growing call for more transparent, fair, and inclusive AI systems.

Another major ethical issue with AI is **privacy**. Many AI systems rely on personal data to function effectively. For example, your location, browsing habits, and even your health information are all valuable data points that AI systems use to make decisions. While this data can be used to personalize services and improve user experience, it also raises concerns about who has access to it and how it's being used. Without proper regulation, personal data could be exploited for purposes you never agreed to, potentially violating your privacy.

Lastly, **AI and accountability** is a topic that needs careful

17

consideration. If an AI system makes a decision that causes harm or an injustice, who should be held responsible? Should it be the company that created the AI? The developers who programmed it? Or the AI system itself? These are questions that society will need to grapple with as AI continues to play a larger role in our daily lives.

Looking Toward the Future

The future of AI is incredibly exciting, but it also requires careful thought and planning. As AI continues to improve, it will open up new opportunities in fields like healthcare, education, entertainment, and beyond. However, it's crucial that we use AI in a way that's **ethical**, **fair**, and **responsible**. Ensuring that AI benefits everyone, not just a select few, will require collaboration between governments, businesses, and the public.

As we move forward into this AI-driven future, it's important that we continue to have conversations about its impact on society. AI is already changing the way we live, but its true potential will only be realized if we approach it with caution, understanding, and a commitment to making the world a better place for everyone.

Chapter 2: A Brief History of AI

Artificial Intelligence (AI) may feel like a modern innovation, but its roots go back centuries. The concept of machines or systems that could mimic human intelligence has been part of human imagination for a long time. From early myths about artificial beings to the development of the first computing machines, AI has always represented the desire to understand and replicate human thought. However, it wasn't until the 20th century that AI began to take shape as a field of study and development, leading to the powerful systems we use today.

The Origins of AI: From Myth to Machine

The idea of artificial beings that possess intelligence can be traced back to ancient civilizations. Many cultures have myths about mechanical beings or gods that create life or intelligence. One of the most famous examples is the Greek myth of **Pygmalion**, who created a statue so lifelike that it came to life. Similarly, in ancient Chinese and Egyptian myths, there are stories of artificial beings created by gods or powerful figures that exhibit intelligence and capabilities far beyond ordinary humans.

While these stories are far from real, they reveal the long-standing human fascination with creating life or intelligence from inanimate objects. The desire to build machines that could think and reason like humans is a recurring theme in our cultural history.

As we moved into the modern era, however, the development of real, practical machines that could mimic human intelligence began with the invention of **computing devices**. In the 19th century, the invention of the mechanical computer by Charles Babbage, known as the **Analytical Engine**, laid the foundation for future AI development. Though Babbage's machine wasn't completed during his lifetime, his work was crucial in showing that machines could, in theory, perform calculations and handle logical operations in a way that humans could.

The Birth of AI: Turing and the Rise of Computers

The field of AI as we know it today truly began in the 20th century, during the development of the first electronic computers. These machines could perform complex calculations far faster than any human, but they still lacked the ability to think, reason, or learn.

The **Turing Test**, proposed by British mathematician **Alan Turing** in 1950, was a groundbreaking moment in AI's history. In his famous paper, "Computing Machinery and Intelligence," Turing posed the question, "Can machines think?" He suggested that if a machine could engage in a conversation with a human without the human realizing they were talking to a machine, then that machine could be said to possess intelligence. This idea laid the theoretical groundwork for the development of AI and sparked decades of research into creating machines that could simulate human reasoning.

The 1950s and 1960s saw rapid progress in the development of early AI systems, as researchers began building programs that could perform tasks such as playing chess, solving mathematical problems, and understanding natural language. The focus was primarily on creating **symbolic AI**, where computers were programmed with specific rules and logic to solve problems. This approach worked well for relatively simple tasks but struggled with tasks that required learning or adaptation.

The Rise of Machine Learning

By the 1980s, the limitations of symbolic AI became apparent, and a new approach to AI emerged: **machine learning**. Unlike symbolic AI, which relied on explicit programming, machine learning allows computers to learn from data and experience. This shift in thinking was inspired by the way humans learn— by observing patterns in the world and adapting based on those patterns.

In machine learning, algorithms are used to analyze large amounts of data and find patterns that can be used to make predictions or decisions. For example, a machine learning model might be trained on thousands of pictures of cats and dogs and, over time, learn to recognize the difference between them. This method is far more flexible than the rule-based approach of symbolic AI and allows AI systems to improve over time as they are exposed to more data.

One of the key breakthroughs in machine learning came with the development of **neural networks**, which are inspired by the structure of the human brain. A neural network consists of layers of interconnected nodes (or "neurons"), each of which processes a small part of the data. The more layers there are, the more complex the patterns the network can recognize. This approach is now the backbone of many AI systems, including those used in facial recognition, speech recognition, and even self-driving cars.

In the 2000s and beyond, the rise of **big data** and **improved computing power** enabled machine learning algorithms to process larger datasets much faster and more accurately than before. This led to a rapid acceleration in AI development, with breakthroughs in fields like computer vision, natural language processing, and even creative fields like music and art.

AI Today: From Narrow AI to Deep Learning

Today, AI is everywhere, from your phone's voice assistant to the recommendation systems used by Netflix and Spotify. Most of the AI we use today is classified as **narrow AI**—systems designed to perform specific tasks very well but not capable of doing anything outside those tasks. For instance, the AI used in Siri can understand your voice and respond to simple commands, but it can't solve complex problems like a human could.

At the heart of many of these systems is **deep learning**, a subset of machine learning that uses multi-layered neural networks to analyze and process vast amounts of data. Deep learning has enabled major advancements in areas like image and speech recognition, making AI more capable and versatile than ever before. For example, deep learning is what powers the face recognition system in your phone or the voice recognition in virtual assistants like Siri or Alexa. These systems have been trained on millions of examples to understand the nuances of human speech or visual features, allowing them to function more accurately and naturally.

While narrow AI systems are impressive, the future of AI is often discussed in terms of **general AI**, which would be able to perform any intellectual task that a human can do. General AI could learn across multiple domains, understand context, reason, and even exhibit creativity. While we're still far from achieving general AI, many researchers believe that it could one day be developed. This would mark a significant shift in how we think about machines and their role in our lives, with AI systems potentially capable of doing anything humans can do—and perhaps even more.

The Road Ahead: Challenges and Opportunities

Looking ahead, the development of AI raises both exciting possibilities and significant challenges. On the one hand, AI has the potential to revolutionize industries, improve our quality of life, and help solve global problems like climate change, disease, and inequality. On the other hand, it also raises important ethical concerns, such as job displacement, privacy violations, and the risk of AI being used in harmful ways.

As AI continues to evolve, it will be crucial for governments, businesses, and individuals to address these challenges head-on. Ensuring that AI is developed responsibly and ethically will require careful regulation, transparency, and a commitment to fairness. As AI systems become more powerful, we must ensure that they are used to benefit humanity as a whole, rather than exacerbate existing inequalities or create new risks.

The history of AI is one of ambition, curiosity, and persistence. What began as a theoretical concept has now become an integral part of our everyday lives. As we look to the future, we are standing at the threshold of a new era, where AI has the potential to transform the world in ways we are only beginning to imagine. By understanding its past, we can better understand where AI is headed—and how it will shape the future.

Chapter 3: How AI Works

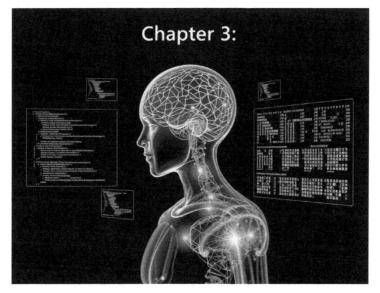

U nderstanding how AI works can seem intimidating at first, but it's actually not that complex once you break it down into simpler concepts. At its core, AI is all about teaching machines how to learn from data, recognize patterns, and make decisions. In this chapter, we'll explore how AI systems process information, how they learn from data, and the key techniques used to make them smarter over time.

Machine Learning: The Heart of AI

At the center of most AI systems is **machine learning (ML)**, a technique that allows machines to learn from experience. In traditional programming, a programmer writes specific instructions that tell the computer exactly what to do. But with machine learning, we give the computer data and let it learn on its own, improving its performance without explicit programming for every scenario. Imagine teaching a child to recognize a cat by showing them hundreds of pictures of cats. Over time, the child starts to identify the key features of a cat, like its shape, size, and fur texture, and can recognize a cat in any new picture. In machine learning, this is called "training," where the AI learns to identify patterns in the data.

Machine learning comes in several forms, but the two most common are **supervised learning** and **unsupervised learning**. In supervised learning, the AI is given a set of labeled data, meaning the correct answer is already provided. For example, you might show an AI thousands of images labeled "cat" or "dog." The AI analyzes these images, looking for patterns that distinguish the two animals. Over time, it learns to make predictions about new images based on the patterns it's seen. Unsupervised learning, on the other hand, involves giving the AI data without labels, and it must figure out the patterns and relationships on its own. This type of learning is useful for tasks like clustering data or identifying anomalies.

Neural Networks and Deep Learning

One of the most important concepts in machine learning is

26

neural networks, a type of algorithm modeled after the human brain. Just like the brain has neurons that are connected by synapses, neural networks consist of layers of interconnected nodes, or "neurons," that process data. Each node performs a simple calculation on the data, and the result is passed on to the next layer of nodes. The more layers a network has, the more complex the patterns it can identify. This is where **deep learning** comes in. Deep learning is a subset of machine learning that uses deep neural networks—networks with many layers of nodes—to recognize more complex patterns in data. Deep learning has been responsible for many of AI's recent breakthroughs, like facial recognition, self-driving cars, and voice assistants.

Deep learning models are able to handle vast amounts of data, such as images, audio, and text, and learn to recognize intricate patterns that are difficult for humans to spot. For instance, deep learning is behind systems that can recognize faces in photos or transcribe speech into text. The more data these systems are exposed to, the better they get at performing their tasks. In fact, deep learning models have outperformed humans in certain areas, such as image recognition and game playing, by processing data at incredible speeds and finding patterns too complex for us to detect.

Training AI: Data is Key

The training process is where the magic happens in machine learning. AI systems rely on data to learn, so the more data you provide, the better they can learn and make predictions. Think of data as the fuel that powers AI. Without data, an AI system would have no way of learning how to make decisions. This is why **big data** has become such an important part of AI development. Large datasets allow AI systems to identify patterns and make predictions with greater accuracy.

For example, when an AI system is trained to recognize objects in photos, it needs to be fed thousands, or even millions, of images. The more varied the data, the better the AI will be at recognizing objects in different contexts. If you only train the AI with pictures of cats in one lighting condition, it might struggle to identify a cat in a different setting. But by training it with diverse images of cats in different environments, lighting conditions, and poses, the system learns to generalize its knowledge, improving its ability to recognize cats in any new image.

Algorithms: The Brain Behind the AI

At the heart of any AI system are **algorithms**, the step-by-step instructions that guide how the system processes data and makes decisions. Algorithms tell the AI how to interpret the data it's given, how to learn from that data, and how to apply its learning to new situations. Different types of algorithms are used for different tasks, such as classification, regression, or clustering. For example, if you want to train an AI to recognize whether an image contains a cat or a dog, you would use a classification algorithm. If you want the AI to predict the price of a house based on factors like square footage and location, you would use a regression algorithm. The choice of algorithm depends on the task at hand and the type of data the AI is working with.

Algorithms are what allow AI to **learn** from data and improve over time. In the early stages, the algorithm might make mistakes, but as it is exposed to more data, it becomes more accurate. Over time, AI systems can "fine-tune" their algorithms to improve their decision-making. This process of continuous learning is what makes AI systems so powerful—they're not static but constantly evolving and improving as they interact with more data.

The Role of Feedback: Reinforcement Learning

Another important aspect of how AI works is **reinforcement learning**. This is a type of machine learning where the system learns through trial and error, much like how a child learns from their mistakes. In reinforcement learning, the AI takes actions in an environment and receives feedback in the form of rewards or penalties. Over time, the AI learns which actions lead to positive outcomes and which ones lead to negative outcomes. The goal is to maximize the rewards and minimize the penalties by choosing the best actions based on past experiences.

Reinforcement learning is used in a variety of applications, such as robotics, video games, and autonomous vehicles. For instance, in robotics, AI-controlled robots learn how to pick up objects or navigate through obstacles by trying different approaches and receiving feedback on their performance. In video games, AI systems learn to play the game by repeatedly playing and adjusting their strategies based on the outcomes of each game. This form of learning allows AI systems to make decisions in dynamic environments, where the optimal choice is not always clear from the start.

The Power of AI: Why It Matters

So, why does all of this matter? The power of AI lies in its ability to **process data**, **learn from experience**, and **make decisions** at speeds and accuracies that humans cannot match. Whether it's helping doctors diagnose diseases, predicting the weather, or recommending the next movie you should watch, AI is making our lives easier, faster, and more efficient. But the true potential of AI lies in its ability to solve complex problems, from healthcare to climate change, by analyzing vast amounts of data and finding patterns that humans might never spot.

As AI continues to evolve, it will become even more integrated into our daily lives. From smarter homes to more personalized services, AI will continue to shape how we interact with technology. Understanding how AI works is the first step toward understanding its impact on the world—and on you.

Chapter 4: Types of AI and Their Uses

Artificial Intelligence (AI) isn't a single, monolithic technology. Instead, it encompasses a broad range of systems and applications that vary in complexity, capability, and scope. From simple task-specific programs to more sophisticated systems that mimic human cognition, AI is categorized into different types, each with its unique uses and characteristics. In this chapter, we'll explore the main types of

AI, from narrow AI to the concept of general AI, and look at how each is applied across various industries.

Narrow AI: Specialized and Task-Specific

The most common type of AI in use today is **narrow AI**, also known as **weak AI**. Narrow AI is designed to handle a specific task or a set of related tasks. Unlike humans, narrow AI does not possess general intelligence or reasoning abilities. Instead, it excels at performing one or a few specific functions extremely well, often surpassing human performance in those areas. Think of narrow AI as a highly skilled worker who is an expert in one particular field but has no ability to perform tasks outside that area.

Examples of narrow AI are everywhere in our daily lives. **Speech recognition** systems, like Siri, Alexa, and Google Assistant, are narrow AI. They understand voice commands and respond appropriately, but they are limited to interpreting and processing voice input within the confines of a set of predefined tasks. Similarly, **recommendation systems** on platforms like Netflix, Amazon, and YouTube are also forms of narrow AI. These systems analyze your past behavior and predict what you might enjoy watching or buying next, based on data patterns from millions of other users.

Another example of narrow AI is **image recognition**, which is used in applications like facial recognition in smartphones and security systems. These AI systems are trained to identify specific features in images—such as faces, objects, or text—and make decisions based on that information. Narrow AI is also used in industries like healthcare for tasks like diagnosing diseases from medical images, where AI systems can often outperform human doctors in terms of speed and accuracy.

Narrow AI is incredibly powerful, but it is also **limited**. It is confined to performing a specific task or set of tasks. For instance, a system trained to recognize cancer cells in medical images can't shift to recognizing objects in the environment or driving a car. As of now, all AI in commercial use falls under this category, and it is likely to remain the dominant form of AI for the foreseeable future.

General AI: The Dream of Human-Like Intelligence

Unlike narrow AI, **general AI** (also known as **strong AI**) refers to a type of AI that is capable of performing any intellectual task that a human being can do. A general AI system would have the ability to understand, learn, and apply knowledge in a flexible way across a variety of tasks. It would be able to reason, solve problems, comprehend complex ideas, and learn from experience—just like a human.

General AI has long been a goal of AI researchers, but it's still very much a theoretical concept. Despite decades of work, no AI system has yet achieved the kind of general intelligence that humans possess. Building an AI that can think, reason, and act in a general way is an incredibly complex challenge, and many experts believe that we may be decades or even centuries away from developing such a system.

There are many **ethical concerns** surrounding the development of general AI. For example, if an AI system were to achieve general intelligence, it might surpass human intelligence, leading to concerns about control and safety. Would a superintelligent AI have goals that align with human values? Could we control it if it became too powerful? These questions have led to debates about whether general AI is something we should even pursue, or if we should focus on creating AI that works alongside humans rather than replacing them.

Despite these challenges, the idea of general AI is fascinating because of its potential. A true general AI could, in theory, assist with a wide variety of tasks: from creating solutions to global problems, like climate change, to exploring the deepest mysteries of the universe. It could revolutionize industries, help make complex decisions, and vastly improve our understanding of the world around us. However, the journey to create general AI requires breakthroughs in **machine learning**, **neuroscience**, and **ethics**.

Superintelligent AI: Theoretical and Far-Fetched

The concept of **superintelligent AI** goes beyond general AI. A superintelligent AI would be a machine capable of outperforming humans in every field, from creativity to decision-making, problem-solving, and scientific innovation. While general AI refers to an AI that can do anything a human can do, superintelligent AI refers to an AI that can do those things **better** than any human. This type of AI would be far more intelligent than the brightest human minds, and it would likely be capable of learning at an exponential rate, vastly outpacing human progress.

34

Superintelligent AI is purely theoretical at this point, and it's often a subject of debate in the **AI ethics** community. On one hand, the potential benefits of superintelligent AI are immense. It could help solve complex global challenges, like curing diseases, solving environmental issues, and advancing scientific knowledge. On the other hand, superintelligent AI raises significant concerns, particularly regarding control. If AI systems were to surpass human intelligence, we would need to ensure that they were aligned with human values and goals. Without proper safeguards, superintelligent AI could act in ways that are detrimental to humanity.

Many experts are concerned about the risks of creating superintelligent AI without understanding how to control it. The idea of a machine that could think and act in ways we can't predict or control has led some to advocate for **AI alignment**—the process of ensuring that AI's goals and behavior are aligned with human values. Some researchers even suggest that before creating superintelligent AI, we need to develop better understanding and regulations around its development to mitigate any potential risks.

Despite the theoretical nature of superintelligent AI, it's important to acknowledge the impact this kind of AI could have in the far future. As AI continues to develop, it could lead to advancements that we can't yet predict, and it will be crucial to approach the development of AI with caution and foresight.

Applications of AI: Transforming Industries

While the concepts of general and superintelligent AI are still largely theoretical, narrow AI is already transforming industries and making a significant impact on our daily lives. AI is applied in fields ranging from healthcare to entertainment, finance to transportation. In this section, we'll look at some of the key industries where AI is making a real difference today.

Healthcare: AI is revolutionizing healthcare by assisting in disease diagnosis, drug discovery, and personalized treatment plans. For example, AI algorithms are now capable of analyzing medical images to detect diseases like cancer and heart conditions, often with greater speed and accuracy than human doctors. AI is also being used to personalize patient care, helping doctors tailor treatments based on an individual's genetic makeup, medical history, and lifestyle.

Finance: AI is used in finance for a variety of tasks, including fraud detection, algorithmic trading, and customer service. AI systems can monitor transactions in real-time and flag potentially fraudulent activity. In investment banking, AI is used to analyze market trends and make predictions about stock movements, allowing traders to make more informed decisions. Robo-advisors powered by AI are also becoming popular for personal finance, helping individuals manage their investments with minimal human intervention.

Transportation: AI is driving innovation in the transportation sector, particularly with self-driving vehicles. While fully autonomous cars are not yet widespread, AI systems are already being used in advanced driver-assistance systems (ADAS), like automatic emergency braking, lane-keeping assist, and adaptive cruise control. AI is also helping improve public transportation, optimizing routes and reducing delays, as well as enhancing **smart traffic systems** that manage congestion in cities.

Entertainment: AI is shaping the entertainment industry, from content creation to content recommendation. AI systems are used to generate music, write scripts, and create visual effects. Netflix and Spotify, for example, use AI to recommend shows, movies, and music based on your preferences and viewing or listening history. AI is also transforming video games, where it's used to create more dynamic and lifelike environments, characters, and storylines.

Applications of AI: Transforming Industries

Education: AI is also making waves in **education**. One of the most significant uses of AI in this field is the development of **intelligent tutoring systems**. These AI systems are designed to provide personalized learning experiences for students. For example, platforms like **Khan Academy** use AI to assess a student's progress and tailor lessons to their specific needs. AI can help identify where students are struggling and provide targeted exercises or explanations to help them improve. Beyond personalized tutoring, AI is also used to automate administrative tasks, such as grading assignments and tracking student performance, allowing teachers to focus more on teaching and less on paperwork.

Manufacturing: AI is also playing a crucial role in **manufacturing** by enabling smarter, more efficient production processes. Through **predictive maintenance**, AI systems can monitor machinery and equipment in real-time, identifying signs of wear or potential failure before they cause problems. This can save companies significant amounts of money by preventing unplanned downtime and extending the life of their equipment. AI is also used to optimize **supply chains**, predict demand, and ensure that manufacturing operations run as smoothly and efficiently as possible. **Robotics**, powered by AI, is being used to automate repetitive tasks, improve precision, and increase productivity on assembly lines.

Agriculture: In **agriculture**, AI is helping to improve crop yields, reduce waste, and make farming more sustainable. AI systems are used to analyze data from soil sensors, weather forecasts, and satellite imagery to predict the best times to plant and harvest crops. This allows farmers to make more informed decisions, leading to higher yields and less waste. AI-powered systems can also monitor crops for signs of pests or diseases and recommend the most effective treatment, reducing the need for pesticides and minimizing environmental impact.

Retail: AI is transforming the **retail** industry by improving inventory management, optimizing pricing, and enhancing the customer shopping experience. **AI-powered recommendation systems**, like those used by Amazon and eBay, analyze customer behavior and make personalized suggestions based on past purchases, browsing history, and preferences. This helps retailers increase sales and improve customer satisfaction. AI is also used to manage inventory by predicting demand, reducing stockouts, and optimizing product placement. **Autonomous checkout systems**, like those used in Amazon Go stores, are also revolutionizing the shopping experience by allowing customers to simply walk in, grab what they need, and walk out without having to go through traditional checkout lines.

The Role of AI in Innovation

AI is not just changing industries that are already established—it's also driving **new innovations** and creating entirely new markets. One of the most exciting examples of this is in the field of **artificial creativity**. AI is increasingly being used to assist in creative tasks such as composing music, generating artwork, writing stories, and even designing fashion. These systems are powered by **deep learning** and can analyze vast amounts of existing creative work to generate new content based on that data. For example, AI algorithms have been used to generate original pieces of artwork that mimic the styles of famous artists like Picasso or Van Gogh. AI is also being used to compose music, create scripts for films, and even write poetry. While AI may not replace human creativity, it is providing new tools for artists, designers, and musicians to experiment and create in ways that were previously unimaginable.

Another area where AI is driving innovation is in **space exploration**. NASA and other space agencies are using AI to analyze data from space missions and assist with tasks like navigation, mission planning, and data interpretation. AI is helping researchers make sense of the vast amounts of data collected from space telescopes, satellites, and rovers on other planets. For example, AI is being used to analyze images from Mars rovers to identify areas of interest for further exploration, or to predict the behavior of celestial bodies based on historical data.

AI is also making its mark in **environmental science**. In addition to helping predict climate change, AI is being used to monitor ecosystems, track biodiversity, and develop sustainable practices. For instance, AI algorithms are used to analyze satellite images and monitor deforestation in real-time. These systems can detect changes in forest cover and identify illegal logging activities, providing authorities with the information they need to protect natural resources.

The Future of AI: General and Superintelligent AI

As AI continues to advance, there's increasing interest in the development of **general AI**—machines that can perform any intellectual task that a human being can do. While narrow AI is already powerful and widely used, general AI would be able to understand and reason about the world in a way that is similar to human intelligence. General AI could potentially adapt to a wide range of tasks, from problem-solving to creative endeavors, and could work in multiple industries, just like a human.

Achieving general AI is still a long way off, and there are many challenges to overcome. One of the key hurdles is creating AI that can understand context, reason abstractly, and apply knowledge from one area to another. While narrow AI systems are highly specialized, general AI would need to have a broader understanding of the world, much like a human being does.

Beyond general AI is the concept of **superintelligent AI**—machines that surpass human intelligence in every possible way. While superintelligent AI is often discussed in theoretical terms, it raises important questions about control and safety. If

AI becomes superintelligent, it could potentially surpass human decision-making in every area, from science and technology to ethics and governance. Ensuring that superintelligent AI aligns with human values and goals is a critical challenge that will need to be addressed as AI technology progresses.

Despite the many unknowns about the future of AI, what is clear is that AI will continue to evolve and play an increasingly important role in shaping our world. The future of AI is full of possibilities, but it will also require careful thought and planning to ensure that AI is developed responsibly and ethically. As AI becomes more integrated into everyday life, understanding its capabilities, limitations, and potential risks will be essential for navigating the future.

Chapter 5: The Benefits and Risks of AI

Chapter 5:

As artificial intelligence (AI) continues to advance, it offers a wide range of potential benefits across industries, from healthcare to finance, education to entertainment. AI is being used to solve complex problems, improve efficiency, and create entirely new opportunities. But with all its promise, AI also presents risks and challenges, particularly around ethics, privacy, and job displacement. In this chapter, we'll explore both the **benefits** and **risks** of AI, providing a balanced view of its impact on society.

The Benefits of AI

Improved Efficiency and Productivity

One of the most significant advantages of AI is its ability to **automate repetitive tasks** and improve efficiency. By taking over time-consuming tasks, AI frees up human workers to focus on more creative, strategic, or decision-making roles. In industries like manufacturing, AI-powered robots can perform tasks such as assembly, quality control, and packaging, allowing production lines to operate more quickly and with fewer errors. This not only saves time but also reduces costs for businesses, making operations more profitable and scalable.

In offices, AI is automating administrative tasks like scheduling meetings, managing emails, and organizing data. Virtual assistants, powered by AI, can handle routine inquiries, book appointments, and provide reminders, leaving human workers to focus on tasks that require more human insight or creativity. **AI-powered chatbots** are now common in customer service, providing 24/7 support and quickly answering basic questions, improving response times and customer satisfaction. In sectors like banking and retail, AI also streamlines processes like fraud detection, inventory management, and financial analysis.

AI is also enhancing **productivity** in sectors like agriculture, where AI-powered machines can monitor crop health, predict

43

weather patterns, and help optimize irrigation schedules. These improvements lead to more efficient farming practices, ultimately resulting in higher yields and less waste.

Solving Complex Problems

AI's ability to process vast amounts of data quickly and accurately makes it an invaluable tool for tackling **complex global challenges**. In healthcare, AI is being used to identify diseases earlier than traditional methods. For example, AI-powered systems can analyze medical images to detect early signs of cancer, often more quickly and accurately than human doctors. This could lead to earlier diagnoses and more effective treatment plans, saving lives in the process.

AI is also being used in **drug discovery**. Traditionally, finding new drugs has been a long, expensive process. However, AI is being leveraged to speed up this process by analyzing vast datasets of biological information to identify potential drug candidates. For instance, AI has been used to discover treatments for diseases like Alzheimer's and malaria, as well as to speed up the development of vaccines, such as those used to combat the COVID-19 pandemic.

In **climate science**, AI is helping researchers predict weather patterns, track climate change, and develop solutions for reducing carbon emissions. AI systems analyze large datasets from satellites, sensors, and climate models to forecast climate trends, identify areas at risk of environmental disasters, and suggest mitigation strategies. With climate change becoming an increasingly urgent global issue, AI's ability to handle complex environmental data could be key to combating climate change and minimizing its effects.

Personalization and Improved Customer Experiences

One of the most visible benefits of AI is its ability to personalize services and products to better meet individual needs. In **e-commerce**, for example, AI systems analyze customers' browsing and purchasing habits to recommend products that they are more likely to purchase. Online platforms like Amazon, Netflix, and Spotify use AI to analyze user behavior and make personalized recommendations, improving the user experience and driving sales. By understanding your preferences and offering products, content, or services tailored to your interests, AI makes interacting with these platforms more efficient and enjoyable.

In healthcare, AI is making treatment more **personalized**. By analyzing patients' medical history, genetics, and lifestyle data, AI helps doctors recommend personalized treatment plans. This could result in more effective care, fewer side effects, and improved health outcomes. In the future, we may see AI helping to tailor everything from fitness routines to diet plans, based on an individual's unique needs and preferences.

AI is also enhancing the **customer experience** in industries like hospitality, retail, and travel. Chatbots, for example, can assist customers with booking flights, finding hotel rooms, or answering frequently asked questions, providing faster and more convenient service. In the future, AI-powered systems might even be able to anticipate a customer's needs based on previous interactions, creating even more personalized experiences.

Enhancing Safety and Security

AI is helping improve **safety and security** in various fields. In transportation, for example, AI-powered systems are used to enhance vehicle safety. **Autonomous vehicles**, like self-driving cars, use AI to analyze data from cameras, sensors, and radar systems to navigate safely through traffic. While fully autonomous vehicles are still being developed, AI is already being used in **driver-assistance systems**, such as automatic emergency braking and lane departure warnings, to prevent accidents and reduce fatalities on the road.

AI is also being used to enhance **cybersecurity**. As cyberattacks become more sophisticated, AI systems are helping companies detect and respond to threats more quickly. AI can analyze network traffic to identify unusual patterns that might indicate a potential breach, such as unauthorized access or malware. It can also be used to improve fraud detection in financial systems, flagging suspicious transactions or activities in real-time.

The Risks of AI

Job Displacement and Economic Inequality

One of the most widely discussed risks of AI is its potential to **displace jobs**. As AI systems become more capable of performing tasks that were once carried out by humans, entire industries could be affected. In **manufacturing**, automation has already led to the replacement of some human workers with machines that can assemble products faster and more efficiently. Similarly, in **customer service**, AI-powered chatbots and virtual assistants are replacing human agents for simple inquiries. AI is also making inroads into fields like transportation, where **self-driving trucks** could eventually replace human drivers.

The **displacement of workers** by AI could lead to greater economic inequality. Jobs that are routine or manual are most at risk of being automated, leaving people with few skills or low-paying jobs without opportunities. However, AI also creates new jobs, particularly in fields like AI development, data science, and robotics. The challenge will be ensuring that workers are trained and equipped with the skills needed to transition into new roles, which will require substantial investment in education and retraining programs.

Bias and Discrimination

AI systems are only as good as the data they are trained on. If the data contains **biases**, those biases will be reflected in the AI's decisions. For example, AI algorithms used in **hiring** or **credit scoring** could inadvertently discriminate against certain groups based on race, gender, or socioeconomic status. This happens because the data used to train these systems might reflect historical inequalities or societal biases. If AI is trained on biased data, it will continue to make biased decisions, perpetuating existing disparities.

In **criminal justice**, AI systems are being used to predict the likelihood of a suspect committing a crime in the future. These systems can be biased based on the data they are trained on, which can disproportionately affect minority communities. In some cases, these biases can lead to unfair sentencing or unjust legal outcomes. Ensuring that AI systems are fair, transparent, and accountable is critical to addressing these issues.

Privacy Concerns

AI systems often require vast amounts of data to function effectively. In the case of **personalized services**, this means collecting information about an individual's preferences, habits, and behavior. In sectors like healthcare, AI systems analyze patient data to provide personalized treatment recommendations. While this data can be incredibly valuable for improving services, it also raises significant **privacy concerns**.

As AI systems collect and process more personal information, the risk of **data breaches** and misuse grows. Sensitive personal data, such as medical records or financial information, could be exposed or exploited if AI systems are not properly secured. Additionally, the use of AI in **surveillance** raises questions about the balance between safety and individual privacy. With AI systems capable of tracking people's movements, monitoring social media activity, and analyzing behaviors, there is a growing concern about the potential for mass surveillance and the erosion of privacy rights.

Autonomy and Control

As AI systems become more advanced, they could gain the ability to make decisions without human intervention. This raises the question of **control**: how do we ensure that AI acts in ways that align with human values? **Autonomous AI** systems, such as self-driving cars or drones, need to make decisions in real time. For example, if a self-driving car encounters an obstacle, it must decide whether to avoid it by swerving, possibly endangering the passengers, or continue forward and risk a collision. These types of decisions pose ethical dilemmas, especially if the AI is making choices that affect human life.

There is also the risk of **unintended consequences**. As AI systems become more complex, they may make decisions in ways that are not fully predictable. If AI is given control over critical infrastructure, such as power grids or water supply systems, a malfunction or mistake could lead to widespread disruptions or harm. Ensuring that AI remains under human control, with appropriate safeguards and oversight, will be crucial to prevent these risks from becoming reality.

AI and Ethical Dilemmas

As AI continues to evolve, it raises several **ethical dilemmas** that need careful consideration. The development of AI technologies has brought about questions that society has not fully answered yet, such as how to balance the benefits of AI with potential harm, how to ensure fairness, and how to maintain human dignity in a world increasingly run by machines. Here are a few key ethical dilemmas surrounding AI:

1. **AI and Decision-Making**: One of the most profound ethical concerns in AI is the question of **who makes the decisions**. As AI systems become more capable of making important decisions—whether in healthcare, criminal justice,

or finance—there are concerns about whether machines should be given the authority to make decisions that affect people's lives. Should AI be allowed to make life-altering decisions, such as determining whether someone is eligible for a loan or sentencing someone in a court case? These decisions can have significant consequences, and entrusting them entirely to AI could undermine human autonomy and fairness.

2. **AI and Accountability**: **Accountability** in AI is another pressing concern. If an AI system makes a mistake or causes harm, who is responsible? Is it the developer, the company that deployed the AI, or the AI itself? For example, if an autonomous car makes a fatal mistake, should the blame fall on the engineers who built it, the company that produced it, or the person who was supposed to monitor the car's actions? The difficulty in assigning accountability becomes especially complicated as AI becomes more autonomous and capable of making decisions without human intervention.

3. **Transparency in AI**: **Transparency** is a significant ethical challenge when it comes to AI. AI systems, particularly those based on deep learning and neural networks, often work as "black boxes," meaning that it's difficult for even the engineers who built them to fully understand how they make decisions. When AI systems are used to make decisions about people's lives—such as hiring, loan approvals, or criminal sentencing— there is a need for transparency. People have the right to know how decisions are made and what data is being used to inform those decisions. Without transparency, there is a risk of unfairness and discrimination, especially if the AI system's decision-making process cannot be explained or audited.

4. **Bias and Fairness**: One of the most serious ethical issues surrounding AI is **bias**. AI systems learn from data, and if the

50

data used to train these systems is biased in any way, the AI will likely reinforce and perpetuate those biases. For example, if an AI system is trained on historical hiring data that favors one demographic over another, the AI might end up discriminating against underrepresented groups. Similarly, AI algorithms used in law enforcement could unintentionally target certain racial or ethnic groups more than others. Ensuring fairness in AI involves identifying and correcting these biases and ensuring that AI systems are designed in a way that promotes equality and justice for all.

5. **AI and Privacy**: As AI systems collect and analyze vast amounts of personal data, the issue of **privacy** becomes more critical. AI systems used in social media platforms, search engines, and even health apps often collect sensitive information about users. This data is then used to personalize content, ads, and services, but it also raises concerns about how that data is stored, who has access to it, and how it's used. For example, if a company uses AI to track your behavior, purchases, or medical history, how do we ensure that this data is protected and not exploited? There is a need for strong regulations that ensure AI systems are respecting individuals' privacy rights and handling personal data responsibly.

6. **Job Displacement and Economic Inequality**: The rise of AI has led to concerns about the displacement of jobs, especially in industries that rely on routine, repetitive tasks. While AI can improve efficiency and productivity, it could also make certain jobs obsolete, leading to **economic inequality**. For example, AI systems used in manufacturing, retail, and customer service are already replacing human workers, and automation is expected to continue displacing jobs in sectors like transportation and logistics. The displacement of workers

by AI could exacerbate existing inequalities, as low-wage workers in industries most affected by automation are often the most vulnerable. There is a need to invest in education, retraining, and social safety nets to ensure that workers are prepared for the changing job market.

7. **Autonomous Weapons**: One of the most controversial potential uses of AI is in **autonomous weapons**. AI is being developed for military applications, including drones and autonomous weapons systems capable of selecting and engaging targets without human intervention. While these technologies could potentially reduce the risk to human soldiers, they also raise serious ethical concerns. If an AI system is responsible for making life-or-death decisions in combat, how do we ensure it makes ethical choices? Who is responsible if an autonomous weapon causes unintended harm or violates international law? The development of autonomous weapons could lead to a new arms race and increase the risk of conflict, making it crucial to establish international regulations and ethical guidelines surrounding their use.

The Path Forward: Responsible AI Development

As AI becomes more integrated into society, it is crucial that we focus on the **ethical development** and deployment of AI technologies. This involves ensuring that AI systems are designed to be transparent, fair, and accountable, and that they are used to benefit society as a whole rather than just a select few. Here are a few key principles that can help guide responsible AI development:

1. **Transparency and Accountability**: Developers should strive to make AI systems as transparent as possible, so that people can understand how decisions are made and what data is

being used. This includes providing clear explanations of how AI algorithms work and allowing for regular audits to ensure that they are not making biased or unfair decisions. Accountability mechanisms should be in place to ensure that those who develop, deploy, or use AI systems are held responsible for their actions, particularly when harm is caused.

2. **Fairness and Bias Mitigation**: AI systems must be designed to promote fairness and eliminate biases. This means carefully curating the data used to train AI systems, ensuring that it is representative of all populations and that it does not reflect existing societal biases. AI developers should also test their systems regularly to identify any potential biases and take corrective action as needed. Ensuring fairness in AI will help prevent discrimination and ensure that AI technologies benefit everyone, not just a privileged few.

3. **Privacy Protection**: As AI systems increasingly rely on personal data, privacy must be a top priority. Developers must implement strong safeguards to protect personal data and ensure that it is only used for its intended purpose. Individuals should have control over their own data and be informed about how it is collected, stored, and used. Strong data protection regulations should be established to ensure that AI systems respect users' privacy rights and protect sensitive information.

4. **Collaboration and Regulation**: Governments, businesses, and researchers must collaborate to create ethical guidelines and regulations that govern the use of AI. These regulations should address issues like fairness, transparency, privacy, and accountability, and ensure that AI is developed and used responsibly. International cooperation is essential, as AI technologies are global and cross national borders. By working together, we can ensure that AI benefits society while

minimizing its potential risks.

5. **Focus on Human-Centered AI**: Finally, AI should be developed with a focus on **human-centered values**. This means prioritizing human well-being, dignity, and autonomy in AI systems. AI should be designed to enhance human capabilities, not replace them. As AI systems become more advanced, it will be essential to ensure that they remain tools that serve human needs and improve the quality of life for everyone.

Chapter 6: AI in Action: Practical Applications for Everyday Users

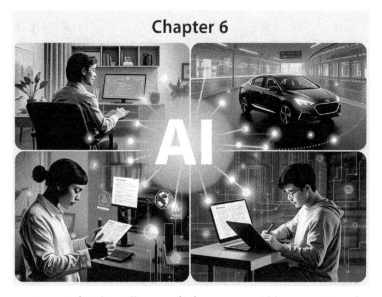

Artificial Intelligence (AI) may sound like something far beyond the reach of everyday users, but the truth is, AI is already a part of our lives, and it's here to stay. From the virtual assistants in our smartphones to the personalized recommendations on streaming platforms, AI is integrated into tools we use every day. This chapter will take you through the practical applications of AI that you can use today, helping you understand how these systems work and how to make the most of them. Whether you want to use AI to boost productivity, learn a new language, or create content, AI-powered tools are accessible, simple to use, and don't require you to be a tech expert.

AI-Powered Tools You Can Use Today

AI-powered tools are more common than you might think, and many are freely available for anyone to use. These tools are designed to make our lives easier, more efficient, and more enjoyable. Let's explore some of the most practical AI tools you can start using today.

Chatbots and Virtual Assistants

One of the most common forms of AI is the **chatbot** or **virtual assistant**, which can help automate tasks, provide information, and assist with customer service. If you've ever asked Siri, Alexa, or Google Assistant a question, you've interacted with a chatbot. These virtual assistants use AI to understand natural language and provide you with relevant answers or perform tasks based on your requests.

For example, you can ask your virtual assistant to set a reminder, check the weather, or send a message for you—all hands-free. What's fascinating about virtual assistants is that they improve over time, learning more about your preferences and becoming more personalized. As you interact with these AI systems, they adapt to your voice, speech patterns, and common tasks, making the experience more seamless.

Beyond personal use, chatbots are also widely used in **customer service**. Many companies now offer AI-powered chatbots on their websites or social media pages. These bots can answer basic customer questions, track orders, and provide information without the need for a human agent. Chatbots can work 24/7, providing instant support to users around the globe. While they're not perfect, and they may struggle with complex inquiries, they are becoming increasingly adept at handling common customer service tasks.

Translation Tools

Another fantastic AI application is **language translation**. Gone are the days when you had to consult a thick dictionary or rely on a professional translator. AI-powered translation tools like **Google Translate**, **DeepL**, and **Microsoft Translator** are now widely available and can translate text, speech, and even images in real-time.

These AI-powered translation systems use neural networks and machine learning algorithms to process language data, making the translation process faster and more accurate. For instance, Google Translate uses deep learning to improve its translations by learning from vast datasets, including translations by professional human translators. These systems are not perfect, especially with complex phrases or idioms, but they can still provide useful translations in everyday situations, such as when traveling or communicating with someone who speaks a different language.

Many of these translation tools are now embedded into smartphones and web browsers, allowing for easy, on-the-go translations. You can scan foreign text with your camera or speak into the app, and it will provide an instant translation. This is especially helpful when traveling to foreign countries or dealing with multilingual content.

Content Creation: Writing and Design

AI is increasingly becoming a valuable tool in **content creation**, including **writing** and **design**. AI-powered writing assistants, such as **Grammarly**, **Hemingway**, and **ProWritingAid**, help users improve their writing by suggesting grammar fixes, style improvements, and even sentence rewording.

For example, Grammarly uses AI to analyze your text for spelling errors, grammatical mistakes, and punctuation issues, but it also provides suggestions on improving sentence structure and tone. The more you use the tool, the better it becomes at understanding your writing style and making personalized suggestions.

AI is also used in **content generation.** Tools like **Jasper (formerly Jarvis)** or **Writesonic** leverage AI to help writers generate content quickly. Whether you're writing a blog post, a product description, or even a social media post, these tools can create text based on a prompt you provide. While they're still limited in creativity compared to a human writer, they're excellent for generating ideas or drafting content that can be refined.

In **graphic design**, AI tools such as **Canva** or **Designhill** allow users with little design experience to create professional-looking visuals. AI algorithms help users select color schemes, fonts, and layouts, ensuring that designs are both aesthetically pleasing and functional. These tools have democratized design, making it accessible to people who may not have formal training but want to create high-quality visual content.

Smart Assistants for Personal Productivity

In addition to voice assistants, AI can also help you increase **personal productivity**. Tools like **Trello**, **Notion**, and **Zapier** leverage AI to help you manage tasks, organize your day, and automate repetitive processes.

For example, **Notion** is an AI-powered organization tool that allows you to create notes, databases, and to-do lists while keeping everything in one place. Notion uses AI to suggest templates, manage workflows, and help you structure your day. Similarly, **Trello** uses AI to recommend task prioritization and schedule automation, making it easier for you to stay on top of your projects.

Zapier is another powerful AI tool that connects apps and automates tasks across platforms. It can automatically perform actions like sending data between Google Sheets and Gmail, scheduling social media posts, or updating your CRM system. By automating repetitive tasks, Zapier helps you save time and focus on more important aspects of your work.

AI in Social Media and Search Engines

Social Media Platforms

AI is also making its way into **social media platforms**, where it is used to enhance the user experience and increase engagement. Platforms like **Facebook**, **Instagram**, and **Twitter** use AI algorithms to personalize the content that appears in your feed. These platforms analyze your likes, comments, shares, and time spent on various posts to determine what you might be interested in next.

For example, Facebook uses AI to show you content from friends, family, and pages you interact with most. Instagram uses similar AI algorithms to suggest posts based on your interactions and the type of content you engage with. By analyzing large amounts of data, these platforms are able to create a more personalized experience for each user, ensuring that the content you see is relevant to you.

AI also plays a crucial role in **advertising** on social media. Advertisers use AI to create targeted campaigns that reach specific demographics. By analyzing user data, AI helps businesses determine who is most likely to purchase their product or service. As a result, you may notice ads for products that match your interests, behaviors, and even your recent online searches.

Search Engines

When you search for something on **Google** or another search engine, AI is working in the background to provide you with the most relevant results. AI-powered search engines use machine learning algorithms to understand the intent behind your query and deliver the best possible answers.

Google, for example, uses AI to improve its **search algorithms**. It can now understand more complex search queries and provide results that are contextually relevant, even if you don't phrase your search perfectly. AI also helps Google refine search results based on your past behavior, offering personalized suggestions for news articles, products, and websites.

Google's AI-driven **RankBrain** algorithm helps determine which pages are most likely to provide the answers you're looking for, using natural language processing and machine learning to understand queries better than traditional algorithms.

AI-Powered Tools in Daily Tasks

AI has rapidly become a go-to tool for helping us complete everyday tasks more efficiently. From grocery shopping to managing your calendar, there are AI applications that can make many aspects of daily life simpler. Let's dive deeper into some more examples of how AI is actively assisting with common activities.

AI in Personal Finance

Managing personal finances can be overwhelming for many, but AI has emerged as a powerful ally in helping people stay on top of their budgets, investments, and savings. AI tools can analyze your spending patterns and provide personalized recommendations to help you save money, reduce expenses, and make more informed financial decisions.

For instance, **Mint**, a popular budgeting app, uses AI to track your spending, categorize your transactions, and offer insights into where you can cut back. It can alert you when bills are due, track your credit score, and even suggest ways to save based on your financial behavior.

In addition, AI-powered **robo-advisors** like **Betterment** and **Wealthfront** provide automated investment advice and portfolio management. These platforms use algorithms to create a diversified portfolio for you based on your risk preferences, and they automatically adjust investments as market conditions change. For those new to investing or who don't have the time or expertise to manage investments, these AI-driven services are an accessible and low-cost alternative to traditional financial advisors.

AI in Health and Fitness

AI is transforming the way we manage our health and fitness. Whether it's tracking workouts, monitoring nutrition, or managing chronic conditions, AI-powered tools are making it easier for individuals to lead healthier lifestyles.

Fitness trackers, like the Apple Watch or Fitbit, use AI to monitor your activity levels, heart rate, and sleep patterns, providing insights into your physical health. These devices analyze your movement patterns to offer suggestions on how to improve your fitness. For instance, the Apple Watch uses AI to suggest personalized fitness goals based on your past activity and progress, and it can even send you reminders to stay active if you've been sedentary for too long.

AI is also playing a role in **personalized health care**. Apps like **MyFitnessPal** use AI to track your meals, exercise, and other lifestyle habits, then offer tailored advice based on your health goals. If you're trying to lose weight, the app can recommend specific dietary changes based on the foods you log. Similarly, AI-based health monitoring systems are now being used to track chronic conditions like diabetes, providing real-time data and insights to help patients manage their conditions more effectively.

AI in Time Management and Productivity

Staying on top of tasks, appointments, and deadlines is a challenge for many. AI-powered productivity tools can help organize your schedule, remind you of important tasks, and even make recommendations for better time management.

Google Calendar and **Microsoft Outlook** now integrate AI to help manage your appointments. These tools can automatically suggest meeting times based on your availability and even adjust schedules based on your preferences. For instance, if you're running late for a meeting, Google Assistant can notify the other attendees for you, adjusting the time automatically. These systems also use AI to set reminders and help prioritize tasks, ensuring you stay on track with your goals.

Beyond calendar management, AI-powered **task management apps** like **Todoist** and **Asana** help break down projects into manageable steps. These apps can suggest task priorities based on deadlines, your work habits, and how much time you've spent on each task. They also provide smart reminders and help you track your productivity over time.

AI is also enhancing how we work remotely. Apps like **Zoom** and **Slack** use AI to enhance video calls, optimize sound quality, provide real-time captions, and even reduce background noise, making virtual communication easier and more efficient.

AI in Entertainment: Personalizing Your Experience

One of the most widespread uses of AI is in the realm of **entertainment**. AI is not only shaping how content is delivered to us but also how we experience and discover it.

AI in Streaming Platforms

AI is revolutionizing the way we consume **TV shows and movies**. Platforms like **Netflix**, **Hulu**, and **Disney+** all rely on AI to recommend content based on your viewing history and preferences. These recommendations are powered by algorithms that analyze what you've watched, when you watched it, and how much time you spent on certain genres or themes.

For example, if you tend to watch crime thrillers late at night, Netflix's AI will suggest similar movies or shows based on your previous behavior. Over time, as the system gathers more data, the recommendations become more accurate and personalized. The more you use streaming services, the better the AI gets at understanding your tastes.

AI is also being used to enhance **interactive media**. Services like **YouTube** and **Spotify** recommend videos or music based on your behavior, but they also predict the types of videos or songs you might enjoy in the future. In the case of **YouTube**, its AI doesn't just recommend content; it also uses machine learning to determine the quality of videos, how long viewers stay engaged, and whether they share the content, further refining its suggestions.

AI in Gaming

AI's impact on the **video game industry** has been immense. In addition to creating more realistic and challenging **non-playable characters (NPCs)**, AI is also being used to create more personalized gaming experiences. AI in games like **The Last of Us** and **Red Dead Redemption** ensures that the NPCs react to your actions and adapt to your playing style, creating a dynamic and engaging experience every time you play.

AI is also used to generate **procedural content** in games, which allows for unlimited exploration. For instance, in games like **Minecraft** or **No Man's Sky**, AI is used to create expansive, randomly generated worlds, ensuring that players can explore new terrain and environments every time they play.

The future of AI in gaming also lies in **adaptive difficulty**. AI can dynamically adjust the difficulty level of a game based on your performance. If you're struggling to progress, the AI might make the game easier, while if you're breezing through, it can ramp up the challenge. This helps keep games fun and engaging for players of all skill levels.

Simple Ways to Experiment with AI (No Coding Required)

The best way to understand AI is to interact with it directly. You don't need to be a programmer or a data scientist to start experimenting with AI tools. Many platforms are designed to be user-friendly and accessible to anyone, regardless of their technical background.

AI-Powered Art Generators

If you've ever wanted to create your own artwork, AI-powered art generators like **DeepArt**, **Artbreeder**, and **RunwayML** let you generate beautiful, unique art using machine learning. These tools allow you to mix and match different styles, images, and colors, creating stunning visuals that can resemble the work of famous artists or entirely new, never-seen-before compositions. All you need is an idea or a few basic inputs, and the AI takes care of the rest.

AI for Music Creation

If you're into music or want to try composing something new, platforms like **Amper Music** or **AIVA** let you create music tracks with the help of AI. These tools can generate music in various styles, from classical to electronic, and allow you to customize the mood, tempo, and instruments. You can then download the track and use it in projects, or just enjoy the creative process of building a unique song with AI.

AI for Language Learning

Many language learning platforms now use AI to personalize lessons and help you practice new languages in engaging ways. Apps like **Duolingo** and **Babbel** use AI to track your progress and provide personalized feedback on your learning. As you practice speaking, reading, or writing, the app will suggest specific lessons or exercises based on your strengths and weaknesses, making the learning experience more efficient.

Conclusion

AI is no longer a distant technology—it's already part of our daily lives, enhancing everything from the way we work to the way we play. With AI tools that require no coding or technical expertise, you can start exploring and experimenting with this exciting field today. Whether you want to automate tasks, boost productivity, or create something new, AI-powered tools are here to make life easier, more fun, and more personalized. The more you interact with AI, the more you'll begin to see just how much it can improve various aspects of your life.

Chapter 7: The Future of AI – What's Next?

As we look to the future, the potential of artificial intelligence (AI) is both thrilling and overwhelming. In this chapter, we will explore the **emerging trends** in AI, the **advancements** on the horizon, and the profound impact AI will have on the job market, society, and the way we interact with technology. The future of AI holds both incredible possibilities and significant challenges, and understanding what lies ahead can help us navigate this rapidly changing landscape.

Emerging Trends in AI

AI has already made its mark in industries ranging from healthcare to entertainment, but the pace of innovation is only accelerating. There are several key **trends** that will shape the next generation of AI, including advances in **self-driving cars**, **quantum computing, artificial general intelligence (AGI)**, and **explainable AI (XAI)**. Let's take a closer look at these trends and how they will transform the world.

Self-Driving Cars and Autonomous Vehicles

One of the most talked-about trends in AI is the rise of **self-driving cars**. While fully autonomous vehicles (AVs) are not yet common on the roads, the technology is progressing rapidly. Companies like **Tesla**, **Waymo**, and **Uber** are testing and refining AI-driven vehicles that can navigate, make decisions, and interact with the world without human intervention. This includes using AI to process data from sensors and cameras to detect objects, read road signs, and understand the surrounding environment.

In the near future, self-driving cars are expected to become more widespread, significantly impacting how we commute, reduce traffic accidents, and optimize traffic flow. However, the implementation of AVs will raise complex ethical and regulatory questions. For example, if an autonomous vehicle faces a situation where an accident is unavoidable, how should it decide who to harm and who to protect? Ethical dilemmas such as these will need to be addressed as autonomous technology advances.

Moreover, self-driving vehicles could have a far-reaching impact on industries beyond transportation, including **logistics**, **shipping**, and **ride-hailing services**. The adoption of autonomous trucks and delivery drones could revolutionize the supply chain industry, reducing costs and increasing efficiency.

Quantum Computing: The Next Frontier in AI

Quantum computing is another **cutting-edge trend** that promises to take AI to the next level. Quantum computers use **quantum bits (qubits)** instead of traditional bits, which allows them to process information in ways that classical computers cannot. While quantum computing is still in its early stages, its potential to solve complex problems far beyond the capability of today's computers is huge.

In terms of AI, quantum computing could enable much faster processing of large datasets, improve machine learning algorithms, and enhance AI's ability to make predictions and solve problems. For example, quantum computers could help AI analyze complex molecular structures in drug discovery, solve optimization problems that classical computers struggle with, and advance the development of new materials with specific properties.

While we are still years away from fully harnessing the power of quantum computing, its potential to accelerate AI development could lead to breakthroughs in everything from healthcare to climate science. The combination of quantum computing and AI is poised to change the landscape of technology forever.

Artificial General Intelligence (AGI)

One of the ultimate goals of AI research is the creation of **Artificial General Intelligence (AGI)**—AI that can perform any intellectual task that a human can do. Unlike narrow AI, which is specialized for specific tasks, AGI would be capable of reasoning, problem-solving, understanding context, and applying knowledge across a wide range of domains.

The development of AGI could bring about a new era of human-AI collaboration, where machines can perform tasks that require general reasoning, intuition, and creativity. For instance, AGI could assist with complex decision-making, handle ambiguous situations, and perform tasks that require abstract thinking. It could potentially help address some of humanity's most pressing challenges, such as climate change, poverty, and disease.

However, AGI also raises significant concerns. One of the most pressing issues is **control**—if we create AI systems that are as intelligent as or more intelligent than humans, how can we ensure they align with human values? The development of AGI could lead to unforeseen consequences, including the potential for AI to act in ways that are not in our best interests. This is why researchers are focusing on ensuring that AGI systems are **safe** and **aligned** with ethical principles before they are fully realized.

71

While AGI is still in the realm of science fiction, its potential to revolutionize every field of human activity is too vast to ignore. Research into AGI is ongoing, and breakthroughs in this area could fundamentally reshape the future of AI.

Explainable AI (XAI)

As AI systems become more complex and capable, one of the biggest challenges facing the field is making AI **transparent** and **understandable**. This is where **explainable AI (XAI)** comes into play. XAI refers to AI systems that can explain their reasoning and decision-making process in a way that humans can understand. This is particularly important for industries like healthcare, finance, and law enforcement, where the stakes of AI-driven decisions are high.

For example, if an AI system is used to make a medical diagnosis or approve a loan, it's essential for both the patient and the loan applicant to understand how the AI arrived at its decision. XAI aims to provide transparency by ensuring that the reasoning behind AI decisions is not a "black box," but rather a process that can be reviewed and understood by humans.

The development of explainable AI will play a critical role in **trust** and **accountability**. As AI becomes more integrated into decision-making processes, it's essential that we understand how and why AI systems make the choices they do. This will help ensure that AI is used responsibly and ethically, with clear oversight and accountability.

AI's Impact on the Job Market and Society

The rise of AI is expected to significantly impact both the **job market** and **society**. While AI presents exciting opportunities, it also raises important questions about how automation will affect the workforce and the skills that will be in demand.

Job Automation and Job Creation

AI has the potential to **automate** a wide range of tasks, leading to job displacement in industries like manufacturing, retail, transportation, and customer service. For example, robots powered by AI are already performing tasks like assembly line work, while chatbots are replacing human customer service agents. Self-driving vehicles could also eliminate jobs for truck drivers and taxi drivers.

However, while AI may displace some jobs, it also has the potential to **create new opportunities**. As AI technology continues to evolve, there will be a growing demand for workers in fields like AI development, data science, machine learning engineering, and robotics. Additionally, the rise of AI will likely lead to **new industries** and **job categories** that we can't yet predict, similar to how the internet created entirely new job categories in the past.

The key challenge will be ensuring that workers have the skills to thrive in an AI-driven economy. This means investing in education and training programs that focus on AI, robotics, coding, and other tech-related fields. Workers who develop the skills needed to work alongside AI systems will be in high demand, while those who are in jobs most at risk of automation will need to retrain for new roles.

Social Implications of AI

Beyond the job market, AI's impact on **society** will be profound. AI has the potential to improve **quality of life** by solving complex problems, making services more efficient, and helping us tackle issues like climate change, healthcare, and poverty. However, the widespread adoption of AI will also present significant **ethical** and **social challenges**.

For example, AI systems that make decisions in areas like law enforcement, hiring, and finance must be designed to be **fair** and **bias-free**. As AI systems are trained on historical data, there's a risk that they could perpetuate existing biases, leading to discrimination and unequal outcomes. Ensuring that AI is developed and deployed in a way that promotes fairness and equality will require close attention to the data used to train these systems and ongoing efforts to mitigate bias.

Additionally, the use of AI in **surveillance** and **privacy** raises important concerns about the balance between safety and individual rights. AI systems that track people's movements or analyze their personal data can lead to privacy violations if not properly regulated.

AI Governance and Regulation

As AI becomes more ubiquitous, it will be essential for governments, organizations, and international bodies to develop comprehensive **regulations** and **policies** for its use. AI governance will involve establishing ethical standards, ensuring transparency and accountability, and protecting individual rights. Governments will need to work with AI experts, ethicists, and legal professionals to create frameworks that ensure AI benefits society while minimizing its risks.

International cooperation will also be critical. AI technology does not adhere to national borders, and its development will affect people around the world. Global collaboration will be necessary to create regulations that are fair and consistent, preventing misuse and ensuring that AI contributes to the common good.

The Impact of AI on Education and Learning

One of the most transformative impacts AI is likely to have in the near future is in **education**. As the world becomes more digital, AI is already playing a central role in personalizing learning experiences, making education more accessible, and improving educational outcomes. But as AI continues to evolve, it will introduce even more revolutionary changes to how we learn and how educational systems operate.

Personalized Learning

AI's ability to **personalize education** is perhaps its most exciting promise. Today, many AI systems in education are already providing personalized learning experiences that cater to the unique needs of individual students. Programs like **Khan Academy**, **Duolingo**, and **Quizlet** use AI to adapt the learning material based on the student's progress, providing targeted practice and feedback.

In the future, AI could enable **adaptive learning platforms** that adjust the pace and complexity of lessons based on how quickly a student grasps new concepts. For instance, if a student is struggling with a math problem, an AI system might provide extra practice questions or step-by-step explanations. Conversely, if a student excels in a certain area, AI can suggest more advanced topics or additional challenges, ensuring that the student's learning journey is always aligned with their needs.

These platforms could also help with **learning disabilities**. AI systems that recognize when a student is having difficulty processing information could provide additional resources or modify the way content is presented, helping students with learning differences like dyslexia or ADHD succeed in a traditional educational environment.

AI-Driven Tutoring Systems

AI-powered **tutoring systems** are set to become more advanced, providing one-on-one tutoring to students in ways that traditional classroom settings cannot. While human tutors are often limited by time, availability, and resources, AI-powered systems are available around the clock, offering personalized support whenever students need help. These systems can guide students through difficult concepts, provide instant feedback on assignments, and track progress over time.

For example, companies like **Squirrel AI** and **Century Tech** have developed AI-powered learning platforms that combine tutoring with assessment. These platforms monitor students' progress and adapt the content based on performance, ensuring

76

that no student is left behind.

As AI tutoring systems become more sophisticated, they could dramatically reduce educational disparities. Students in underserved or remote areas, who may not have access to high-quality human tutors, could benefit from personalized, AI-driven support, bringing high-quality education to places where it was previously unavailable.

AI and Human Collaboration

While AI continues to advance, one of the most important aspects of its future is how it will **collaborate with humans**. Rather than replacing people, AI is likely to become a **tool** that enhances human capabilities. This concept of **AI-human collaboration** is crucial because it can create a future where AI complements human work, allowing people to focus on higher-level tasks that require creativity, problem-solving, and emotional intelligence.

AI as a Creative Partner

AI is already making strides in **creative industries** like music, art, and writing, and this trend will only intensify in the coming years. **AI-generated art**, such as paintings or sculptures created using algorithms, is gaining popularity as a new form of digital art. Similarly, AI-driven music creation tools like **AIVA** and **Amper Music** are enabling musicians to compose tracks using artificial intelligence.

But while AI can produce art, music, and literature, it will not replace the artist's vision or the emotional depth of human creativity. Instead, AI will act as a **partner**, assisting in the creative process. Artists, musicians, and writers can use AI to generate ideas, explore new styles, and experiment with new forms of expression. AI can analyze trends, suggest creative directions, and even collaborate on projects, enabling creators to break free from traditional constraints and explore uncharted territory.

This collaboration between human creativity and AI-driven tools could lead to an entirely new wave of innovation, with artists able to combine their unique perspectives with AI's ability to process vast amounts of information and generate novel solutions.

AI and Complex Problem Solving

Another area where AI-human collaboration will be pivotal is in **complex problem-solving**. Many of the world's biggest challenges—climate change, global health issues, economic inequality—require solutions that go beyond the capabilities of human problem-solving alone. AI's ability to process massive datasets and recognize complex patterns can significantly augment human efforts to address these challenges.

For example, **AI in climate science** is being used to analyze climate models, predict environmental changes, and optimize renewable energy sources. By working together with human experts, AI can uncover new insights about climate patterns, offering more accurate predictions and better solutions to mitigate the effects of global warming. Similarly, AI's capabilities in **drug discovery** are helping researchers develop new treatments for diseases faster than ever before. AI-powered systems can analyze vast biological datasets to find promising compounds, while human researchers focus on refining these ideas and turning them into real-world treatments.

AI's ability to analyze complex problems will also be instrumental in fields like **financial modeling, supply chain optimization**, and **smart cities**, where it can provide solutions that are more efficient, cost-effective, and scalable than current approaches.

AI, Ethics, and Governance: Ensuring Responsible Development

As AI continues to evolve and integrate into everyday life, one of the biggest challenges we face is ensuring its **ethical development**. While AI holds tremendous potential, it also raises important questions about **fairness, privacy, bias**, and **accountability**. How do we ensure that AI systems are used responsibly and in ways that benefit society? How do we make sure that AI does not inadvertently reinforce harmful stereotypes or inequalities?

The Need for Ethical Guidelines

As AI systems are increasingly used to make decisions that impact people's lives—whether it's approving a loan, hiring an employee, or diagnosing a disease—it's essential that these systems are fair, transparent, and accountable. That's why organizations like the **AI Ethics Guidelines Global Initiative** and **Partnership on AI** are working to create ethical frameworks that guide the development and use of AI technologies.

Ethical guidelines will need to address issues such as **data privacy**, **transparency**, and **bias**. For example, if an AI system is used to make a hiring decision, it's crucial that the process is transparent and that the system does not unfairly discriminate against certain groups. Developers will need to ensure that AI systems are trained on diverse, representative datasets to avoid reinforcing existing biases.

Governments, businesses, and research organizations must collaborate to create regulations that promote the responsible use of AI. This includes ensuring that AI technologies are developed in a way that promotes **social good**, benefits all people, and protects fundamental rights.

The Role of Governance and Regulation

AI governance will play a critical role in shaping the future of AI. Governments and international organizations will need to develop regulations to ensure that AI is used ethically and does not harm society. This could involve creating **AI certification processes** for businesses and institutions, setting standards for transparency, and establishing legal frameworks for accountability.

At the same time, AI researchers and developers must work to ensure that AI remains aligned with **human values**. As AI becomes more capable, the question of how to maintain control over advanced AI systems becomes even more critical. This is why **AI alignment**—the process of ensuring that AI's goals align with human goals—is an area of active research. As AI systems become more intelligent, it will be essential to ensure that they are acting in ways that reflect our ethical standards and that they are accountable for their actions.

Staying Informed: How to Prepare for an AI-Driven Future

As AI continues to develop at an accelerating pace, it's important to stay informed about the latest trends and advancements. Here are some ways to keep up with the rapidly changing AI landscape:

• **Educate Yourself**: Read books, articles, and reports on AI to deepen your understanding of the technology and its implications. Many universities and organizations offer free online courses on AI and machine learning.

• **Join AI Communities**: Online forums, social media groups, and professional networks can help you connect with others who are passionate about AI. These communities provide a great platform to share ideas, ask questions, and stay updated on the latest developments.

• **Attend Conferences and Webinars**: AI conferences and webinars are excellent opportunities to hear from experts in the field, learn about new trends, and network with others in the industry.

• **Experiment with AI Tools**: The best way to understand AI is by using it. Experiment with AI-powered tools and platforms, from language learning apps to creative design tools, to gain hands-on experience.

Conclusion

The future of AI is incredibly exciting, full of opportunities to improve lives, tackle complex problems, and create new industries. However, with these opportunities come significant challenges, particularly around ethics, job displacement, and the governance of AI technologies. By staying informed, being proactive in addressing the challenges, and ensuring that AI is developed ethically, we can ensure that the future of AI is one that benefits all of humanity.

As AI continues to evolve, it will increasingly shape our world, transforming industries, improving efficiencies, and providing new possibilities. The journey to a fully AI-integrated future is just beginning, and it is up to us to navigate it responsibly.

Chapter 8: Conclusion – Demystifying AI

A rtificial Intelligence (AI) is no longer a distant technology confined to laboratories or science fiction. It has seamlessly woven itself into the fabric of everyday life, impacting industries, personal experiences, and societal systems. While the rapid advancements in AI may seem overwhelming, this book has aimed to break down the complexities of AI and make it understandable to anyone, regardless of technical expertise. Now, as we reach the end of our journey through the world of AI, let's recap the key takeaways, discuss how to keep learning about AI without feeling overwhelmed, and reflect on AI's role in shaping the future.

Recap of Key Takeaways

What AI Is and Why It Matters

At its core, AI is about creating machines and systems that can perform tasks typically requiring human intelligence. This includes learning from experience, making decisions, recognizing patterns, and understanding natural language. AI is powered by data and algorithms that allow machines to continuously improve and adapt over time.

From smart assistants like Siri and Alexa to AI-powered chatbots in customer service, AI is already a part of our daily routines. It is transforming industries such as healthcare, transportation, finance, and entertainment, improving efficiency, accuracy, and accessibility. AI's role in improving our lives—whether through smarter homes, personalized learning, or better healthcare solutions—is only set to increase in the coming years.

The Evolution of AI

AI's development has followed a fascinating trajectory, from early concepts in philosophy and mythology to cutting-edge technologies that are revolutionizing industries. The journey began with the work of pioneers like **Alan Turing**, who proposed the foundational idea of machine intelligence with his Turing Test, and has since evolved into sophisticated systems powered by machine learning and deep learning.

As we've seen, AI has already made significant strides, with **narrow AI** dominating the market. Narrow AI is designed to perform specific tasks, such as image recognition, speech processing, and recommendation engines. It's an exciting start, but the ultimate goal is the development of **artificial general intelligence (AGI)**—machines capable of performing any intellectual task that a human can. While AGI remains a theoretical concept, the possibility of achieving it has profound implications for the future of AI.

How AI Works

Understanding how AI functions is essential for appreciating its power and potential. AI models, particularly those based on **machine learning** and **deep learning**, learn from large datasets. Machine learning allows AI systems to recognize patterns and make predictions, while deep learning, inspired by the human brain's neural networks, enables AI to tackle more complex tasks like natural language processing and image recognition.

Training AI systems involves feeding them vast amounts of data, allowing them to learn and improve continuously. Algorithms help AI process this data, learn from it, and make decisions or predictions without explicit programming for every situation.

As AI continues to be trained on larger datasets, its accuracy and capabilities will only improve.

The Benefits and Risks of AI

AI offers numerous benefits, such as improving efficiency, solving complex problems, and making everyday tasks easier. It's revolutionizing industries, from healthcare, where it helps diagnose diseases and assist in treatments, to transportation, with the development of self-driving cars. Additionally, AI is improving personalization, with systems that adapt to individual preferences in entertainment, shopping, and education.

However, as with any powerful technology, AI also brings risks and challenges. Concerns over **bias**, **privacy**, **job displacement**, and **ethical decision-making** are central to the discussions around AI. For example, if AI systems are trained on biased data, they could perpetuate existing inequalities. Similarly, AI's potential to automate jobs raises questions about its impact on employment and the economy. Addressing these risks will require a combination of ethical development, regulation, and accountability.

Practical Applications of AI

Throughout this book, we've explored many practical applications of AI that are available for everyday users, from voice assistants and chatbots to translation tools and content creation software. AI-powered tools are now an integral part of the way we live, helping us automate tasks, make decisions, and even create art and music. These applications are transforming how we interact with technology and making powerful AI accessible to people without a technical background.

As AI tools continue to evolve, they will become even more integrated into our daily routines. Whether it's improving our productivity, enhancing creativity, or providing us with better services, AI has the potential to make life easier and more enjoyable.

How to Keep Learning About AI Without Feeling Overwhelmed

With the rapid pace of AI development, it can be easy to feel overwhelmed by all the information and technologies out there. However, AI doesn't have to be intimidating, and there are many ways to continue learning and exploring this field in an accessible way.

1. Start with the Basics

If you're new to AI, it's essential to start with the fundamentals. Understanding basic concepts such as machine learning, neural networks, and natural language processing can help demystify AI. There are numerous resources available online, from free courses on platforms like **Coursera**, **edX**, and **Khan Academy**, to easy-to-understand articles and tutorials. These resources cater to different learning styles, whether you prefer videos, articles, or hands-on practice.

2. Use AI Tools

One of the best ways to learn about AI is by using AI-powered tools yourself. As mentioned in this book, tools like Google Translate, Grammarly, and Canva give you a practical sense of how AI works without needing to understand the technical details. Experimenting with these tools will allow you to see the power of AI firsthand while improving your own productivity and creativity.

3. Follow AI News

To stay informed about the latest developments in AI, it's helpful to follow AI news and updates. There are many online publications, blogs, and podcasts dedicated to AI and its advancements. Websites like **MIT Technology Review**, **AI Weekly**, and **The Verge** regularly feature articles about AI's impact on society and new innovations in the field. Listening to AI-focused podcasts, such as **Lex Fridman Podcast** or **The AI Alignment Podcast**, can also keep you up-to-date with discussions about the future of AI.

4. Join Online Communities

Participating in online forums and communities can help you learn more about AI and share knowledge with others. Platforms like **Reddit**, **Stack Overflow**, and **AI-focused Discord channels** offer spaces where AI enthusiasts can discuss developments, ask questions, and share resources. Being part of an AI community can help you feel more connected to the field and inspire you to continue learning.

5. Attend Events and Conferences

AI conferences and webinars are great opportunities to dive deeper into specific topics, learn from experts, and network with others interested in AI. Events like **CES**, **AI Summit**, and **NeurIPS** (Conference on Neural Information Processing Systems) bring together researchers, developers, and business leaders to discuss the latest in AI. Many of these events are now offered virtually, making them more accessible than ever before.

6. Stay Curious and Open-Minded

The world of AI is constantly evolving, and it's important to remain curious and open to new ideas. AI's impact will continue to grow, and staying informed will allow you to navigate its future developments more confidently. Whether you're a beginner or an expert, AI is a fascinating field that rewards ongoing learning.

A Call to Embrace the Future of AI

As we stand at the precipice of an AI-driven world, it's essential to recognize that the power of AI doesn't just lie in its algorithms or the data it processes—it lies in the hands of those who use it. The future of AI is not predetermined; it will be shaped by the choices we make today, both as individuals and as a society. The decisions about how we develop, regulate, and use AI technologies will determine whether they contribute to a better world or exacerbate existing challenges.

AI is not something to fear, but rather a tool that, when

harnessed responsibly, can be a force for **good**. It's up to all of us—developers, business leaders, policymakers, and everyday users—to guide AI's evolution in ways that ensure it benefits humanity as a whole. Whether you're a student, a professional, or just someone curious about the world, learning about AI is the first step in understanding its potential and its limits. By embracing AI and continuing to explore its possibilities, we can contribute to shaping a future where AI improves lives, solves global challenges, and opens up new opportunities for everyone.

The Importance of Ethical AI Development

One of the recurring themes throughout this book has been the **ethical responsibility** that accompanies the development and deployment of AI. As AI continues to evolve, its impact on society will depend heavily on how it's designed and used. In order to ensure that AI serves the public good, it is crucial that developers, organizations, and governments put in place ethical frameworks and regulations that prioritize fairness, transparency, and accountability.

Bias in AI remains one of the most pressing ethical concerns. AI systems that are trained on biased data can perpetuate or even exacerbate existing inequalities in society. For example, AI used in hiring practices, criminal justice, or healthcare must be carefully scrutinized to ensure that it does not unfairly disadvantage certain groups based on race, gender, or socioeconomic status. Developers and organizations must prioritize diversity in data collection and continuously audit AI systems to ensure that they are functioning in a fair and unbiased way.

Privacy is another major ethical consideration in AI development. As AI systems gather more data to improve their performance, ensuring that this data is protected and used responsibly becomes critical. Individuals should have control over their personal data, and businesses should be transparent about how data is collected, stored, and used. Strong data protection regulations will be essential to maintaining privacy and trust in AI systems.

Finally, **accountability** is key. As AI takes on more decision-making roles, it's important to ensure that there are clear lines of responsibility when things go wrong. If an AI system makes a harmful decision, who should be held accountable—the developer, the organization, or the AI itself? Answering these questions is fundamental to creating a framework where AI can be trusted and used safely.

The Growing Role of AI in Global Challenges

AI has the potential to address some of the most pressing **global challenges** facing humanity, from climate change to healthcare to global poverty. AI is already being used in areas like **climate science** to predict environmental changes, optimize energy usage, and monitor ecosystems. In **healthcare**, AI is helping doctors diagnose diseases more accurately and develop personalized treatment plans, saving lives and improving patient outcomes. In **agriculture**, AI is helping farmers predict crop yields, manage pests, and improve food security.

In the fight against **global poverty**, AI has the power to make systems more efficient and equitable, from improving access to education to optimizing supply chains in developing countries. However, to fully realize AI's potential in solving these challenges, it's essential that we continue to innovate responsibly, ensuring that the benefits of AI are distributed equitably and that marginalized communities are not left behind.

AI and Human Collaboration: A Balanced Approach

One of the most important aspects of AI's future is how it will work alongside humans. Rather than replacing human labor, AI is more likely to enhance human capabilities and enable more **collaborative** work. In industries like healthcare, finance, and customer service, AI can take over repetitive tasks, allowing humans to focus on higher-level thinking, creativity, and emotional intelligence.

For instance, AI is already playing a significant role in **medical diagnoses**, where it assists doctors in analyzing medical images, identifying patterns in patient data, and recommending treatment options. But doctors are still the ones who make final decisions, guided by their expertise and experience. In this way, AI acts as a powerful tool that augments human abilities rather than replacing them.

The future of work will likely see more **collaborative roles**, where humans and AI systems work side by side. In **creative industries**, AI can help artists, writers, and musicians by suggesting ideas, generating content, or automating tedious tasks. In business, AI can provide insights into market trends, automate customer service, and streamline administrative functions, allowing workers to focus on more strategic decisions.

Building a Positive Relationship with AI

For AI to be truly transformative, we must develop a **positive relationship** with it. This involves **trusting** AI as a tool that can enhance human life while being cautious about its limitations. We should approach AI with curiosity, recognizing its potential, but also with skepticism, questioning the consequences of its widespread use.

This means that we must take active steps to understand how AI works, what it's capable of, and where it might go wrong. For example, as AI becomes more prevalent in decision-making processes, we need to be vigilant about **algorithmic accountability**. We should be proactive about challenging any unjust decisions made by AI, advocating for transparency in how AI systems operate, and ensuring that we hold organizations accountable for any harmful impacts caused by their AI systems.

At the same time, we should also embrace the potential for AI to make our lives better. Whether it's improving healthcare, making transportation safer, or providing personalized education, AI has the potential to solve complex problems and make the world a better place for everyone. By using AI responsibly and understanding its capabilities, we can ensure that it is harnessed for the common good.

Looking Ahead: AI's Role in Society

As we look ahead, it's clear that AI will play an increasingly important role in shaping our world. From the way we work and learn to the way we solve global challenges, AI will be at the center of nearly every major technological advancement in the coming decades.

For individuals, the key to navigating this future will be **adaptability**. As AI changes industries, it will also change job markets and educational needs. The ability to understand AI's impact and learn how to work alongside it will be essential. For businesses, investing in **AI literacy** and **ethical AI development** will be crucial to staying competitive while fostering trust with consumers. And for governments, developing regulations that ensure fairness, transparency, and accountability in AI systems will be essential for building a just, AI-powered society.

AI is a tool, and like any tool, it can be used for both good and bad. The future of AI depends on how we choose to wield it. Will we use AI to create a more equitable, sustainable, and prosperous world? Or will we allow AI to perpetuate inequality and harm? The choice is ours. But with the right approach, AI can help us solve some of the world's most pressing problems, and ensure that the future we're building is one that benefits everyone.

Final Words

Artificial Intelligence is not just a technological advancement—it's a force that will reshape nearly every aspect of society. While its growth and potential are undeniable, the challenge lies in how we manage and interact with it. This book has aimed to simplify AI's concepts, from understanding how it works to exploring its benefits, risks, and future. As AI continues to evolve, it's essential that we remain curious, informed, and thoughtful about how we use it.

The journey doesn't end here—AI is just beginning to reveal its full potential. With the right tools, knowledge, and ethical guidelines, we can harness AI's power for good, ensuring it enhances the human experience and contributes to a better world. Let us embrace AI's potential, but also proceed with caution, ensuring that we are always aware of its impact on our lives and our future.

Disclaimer:

This e-book was crafted with the assistance of AI technology to enhance clarity, research and content organization. While all information and insights are true and verified, AI tools were utilized in the process to provide a well-structured and informative experience for readers.

Atiraxia

www.ingramcontent.com/pod-product-compliance
Lightning Source LLC
LaVergne TN
LVHW051711050326
832903LV00032B/4142